PlayTime® Piano

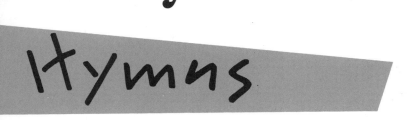
Hymns

Level 1

5-Finger Melodies

Arranged by

Nancy and Randall Faber

Production: Frank and Gail Hackinson
Production Coordinator: Marilyn Cole
Design: Gwen Terpstra
Music Editor: Edwin McLean
Engraving: Music Craft of Hollywood, Inc. (Fla.)

THE
F·J·H
MUSIC
COMPANY
INC.

2525 Davie Road, Suite 360
Fort Lauderdale, Florida 33317-7424

A NOTE TO TEACHERS

PlayTime® Piano Hymns is a collection of favorite hymns arranged for the Level 1 pianist. The arrangements use elementary 5-finger hand positions that reinforce note names and interval recognition. The selections offer excellent supplementary material and they are perfect for Sunday School and church performance.

PlayTime® Piano Hymns is part of the *PlayTime® Piano* series. "PlayTime" designates Level 1 of the *PreTime® to BigTime® Piano Supplementary Library* arranged by Faber and Faber.

Following are the levels of the supplementary library, which leads from *PreTime®* to *BigTime®*.

PreTime® Piano   (Primer Level)
PlayTime® Piano   (Level 1)
ShowTime® Piano   (Level 2A)
ChordTime® Piano   (Level 2B)
FunTime® Piano   (Level 3A – 3B)
BigTime® Piano   (Level 4)

Each level offers books in a variety of styles, making it possible for the teacher to offer stimulating material for every student. For a complimentary detailed listing, write the publisher listed below.

Teacher Duets

Optional teacher duets are a valuable feature of **PlayTime® Hymns**. Although the arrangements stand complete on their own, they sound richer and fuller when played as duets. And not incidentally, they allow the opportunity for parent and student to play together.

Helpful Hints:

1. The student should know his part thoroughly—and be able to play his part up an octave—before the teacher duet is used. Accurate rhythm is especially important.

2. Harmony notes in the student part may be omitted if a steady rhythm is difficult to achieve.

3. Rehearsal numbers are provided to give the student and teacher starting places.

4. The teacher may wish to count softly a measure aloud before beginning, as this will help the ensemble.

ISBN 0-929666-00-3

Revised Edition

TABLE OF CONTENTS

FF1000

4

Middle C Position

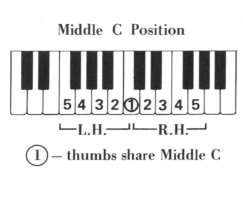

5 4 3 2 ① 2 3 4 5
└─ L.H. ─┘ └─ R.H. ─┘

① – thumbs share Middle C

Jan 3, 2006
Count out loud
Play 4 times a day

Good job!

Jesus Loves Me

Text – Anna Warner
Tune – Wm. Bradbury

Happily

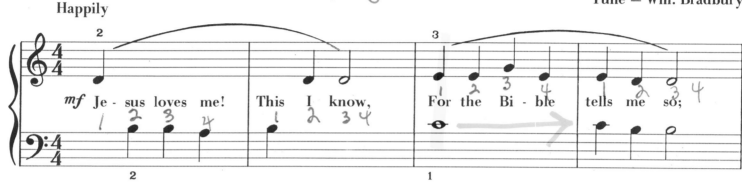

mf Je - sus loves me! This I know, For the Bi - ble tells me so;

Lit - tle ones to Him be - long, They are weak but He is strong.

Teacher Duet: (Student plays 1 octave higher)

R.H.
L.H. *mp* *with pedal*

This arrangement © 1988 by The FJH Music Company Inc.
International Copyright Secured. Made in U.S.A. All Rights Reserved.

FF-1000

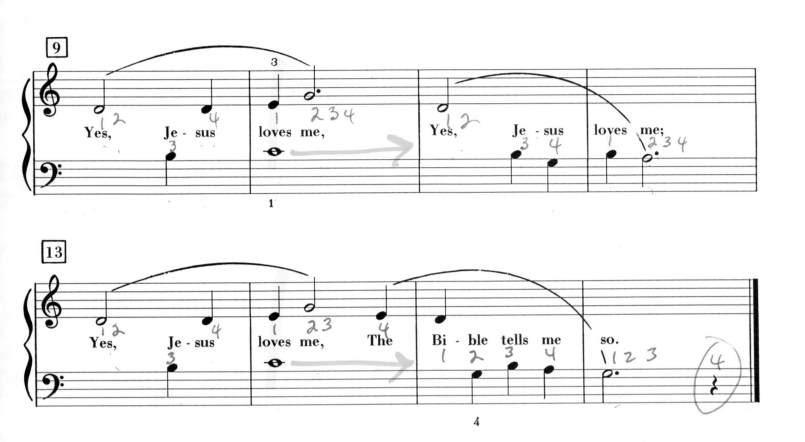

6

Do Lord

Combining Middle C and C Positions

Text — Anonymous
Tune — Spiritual

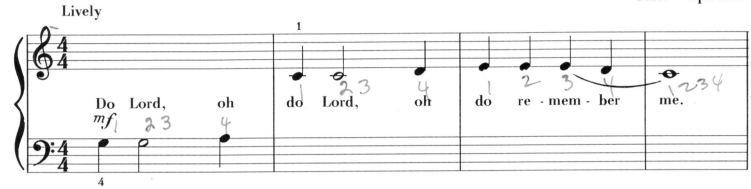

Do Lord, oh do Lord, oh do re - mem - ber me.

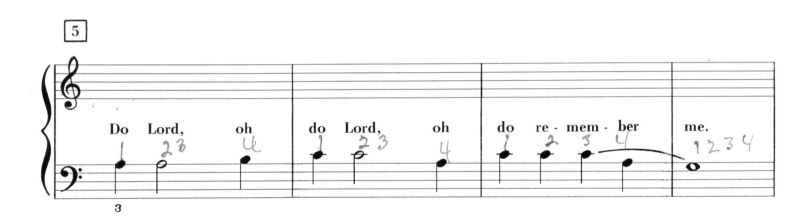

Do Lord, oh do Lord, oh do re - mem - ber me.

Teacher Duet: (Student plays 1 octave higher)

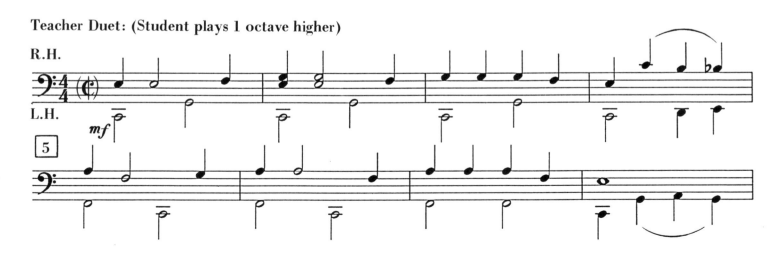

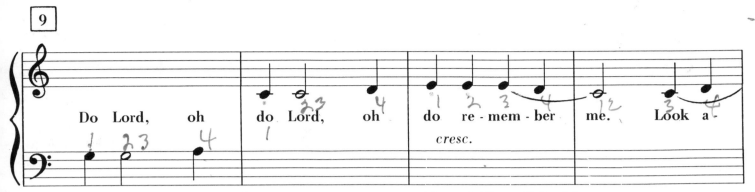

Move L.H. to C Position

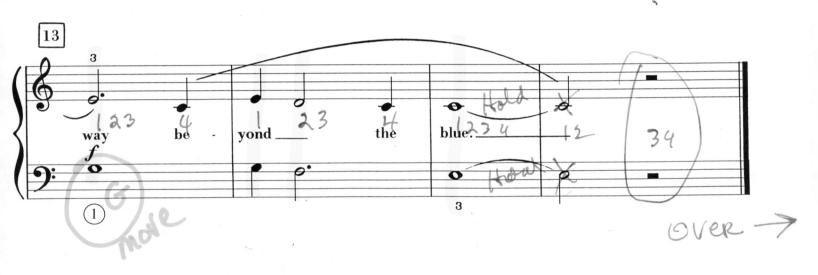

over →

8

Stand Up, Stand Up for Jesus

Combining Middle C and C Positions

Text — George Duffield
Tune — George Webb

Like a march

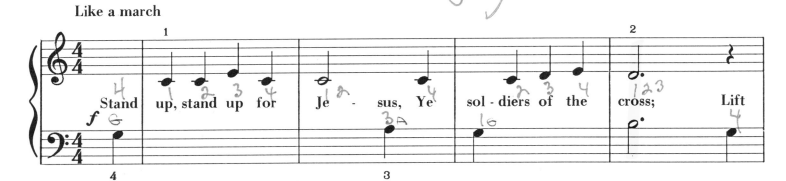

Stand up, stand up for Je - sus, Ye sol - diers of the cross; Lift

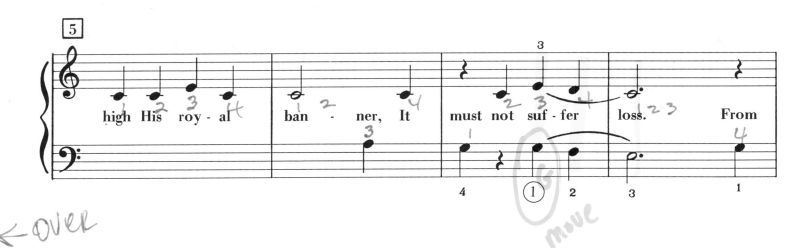

high His roy - al ban - ner, It must not suf - fer loss. From

← *over*

Teacher Duet: (Student plays 1 octave higher)

R.H.

L.H. *mf*

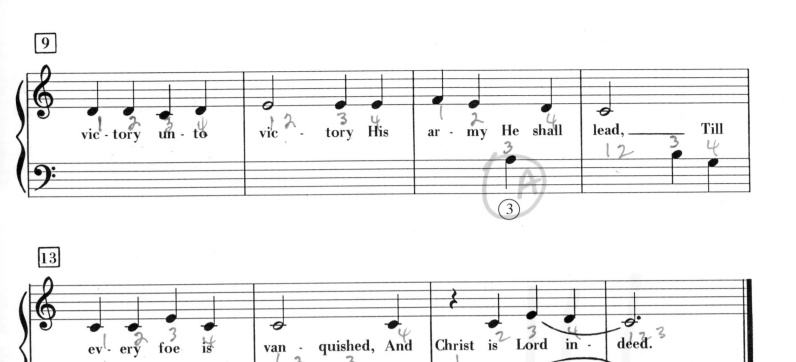

Holy, Holy, Holy

Text — Reginald Heber
Tune — John B. Dykes

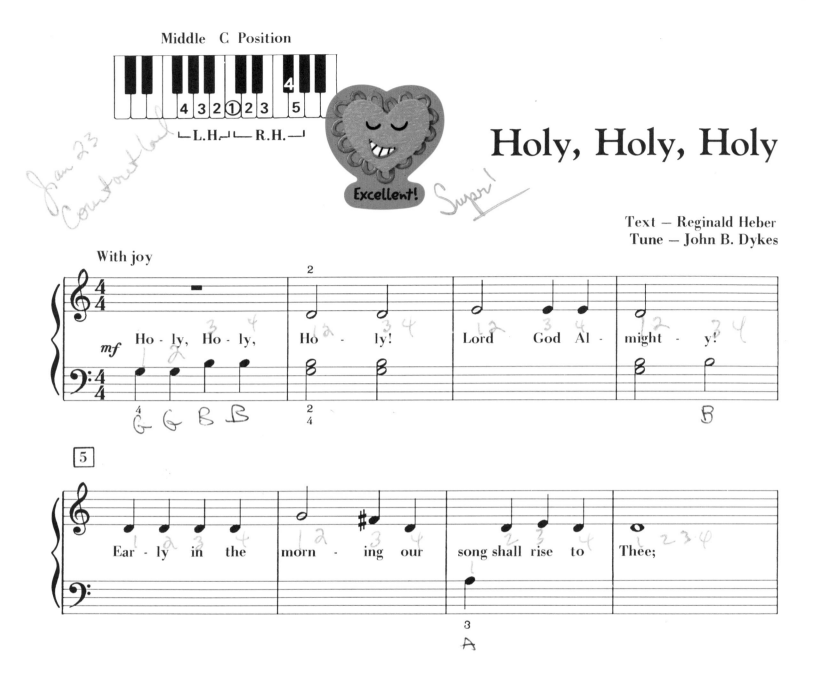

Teacher Duet: (Student plays 1 octave higher)

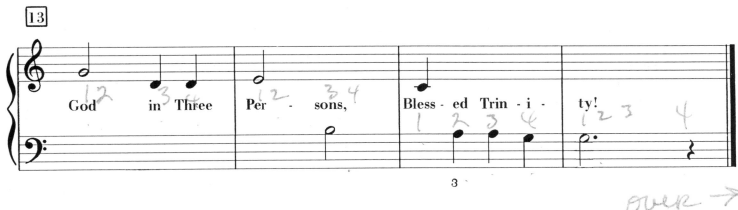

over →

This Little Light of Mine

Text — Anonymous
Tune — Spiritual

14

Fairest Lord Jesus

Text — Munster Gesangbuch
Tune — Silesian Folk Song

Teacher Duet: (Student plays 1 octave higher)

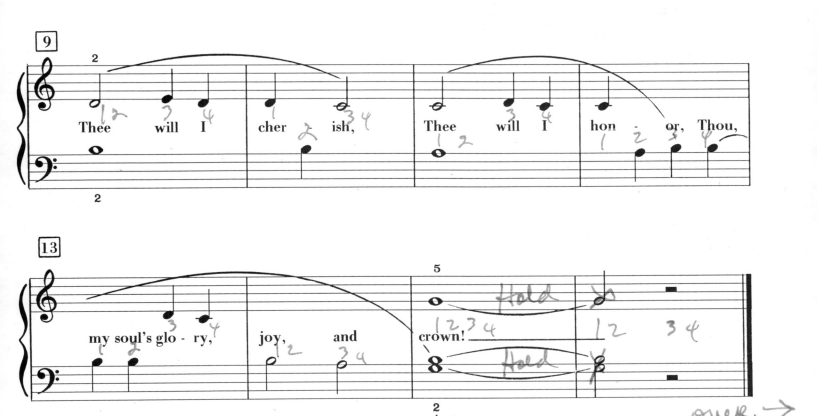

16

C Position

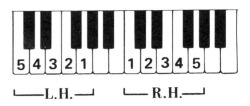

5 4 3 2 1   1 2 3 4 5
└──L.H.──┘ └──R.H.──┘

Joyful, Joyful
We Adore Thee

Text — Henry van Dyke
Tune — Ludwig van Beethoven

With enthusiasm

mf Joy - ful, joy - ful,   we a - dore Thee,   God of glo - ry,   Lord of love;

5   1

[5]

Hearts un - fold like   flowers be - fore Thee,   Open - ing to the   sun a - bove.

Teacher Duet: (Student plays 2 octaves higher)

R.H.

L.H. *mp*

[5]

18

Middle C Position

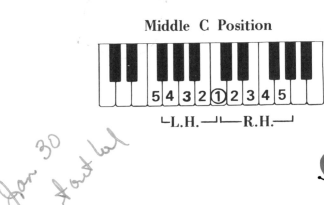

└─L.H.─┘└─R.H.─┘

O Worship the King

xoxo

Text — Robert Grant
Tune — Johann Haydn

Not too fast

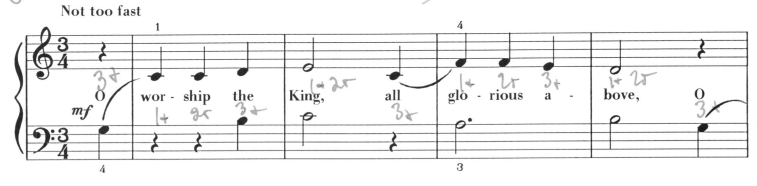

O wor-ship the King, all glo-rious a - bove, O

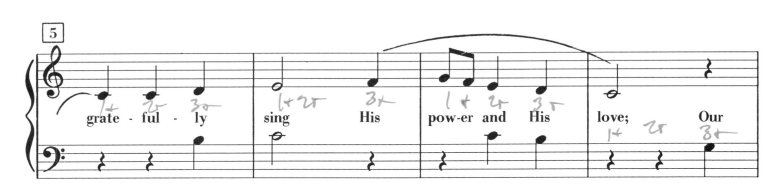

grate-ful-ly sing His pow-er and His love; Our

Teacher Duet: (Student plays 1 octave higher)

This arrangement © 1988 by The FJH Music Company Inc.

FF-1000

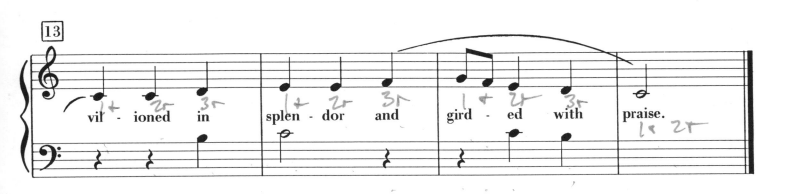

FF-1000

Middle C Position

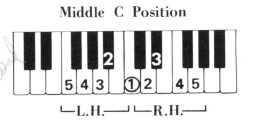

What a Friend
We Have in Jesus

Text — Joseph Scriven
Tune — Chas. Converse

What a friend we have in Je - sus, All our

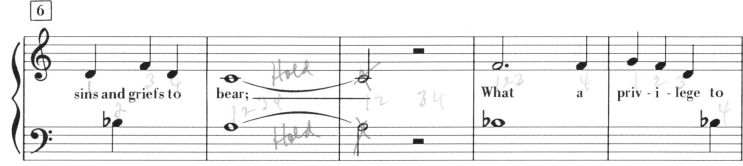

sins and griefs to bear; What a priv - i - lege to

car - ry Ev - ery - thing to God in prayer!

Teacher Duet: (Student plays 1 octave higher)

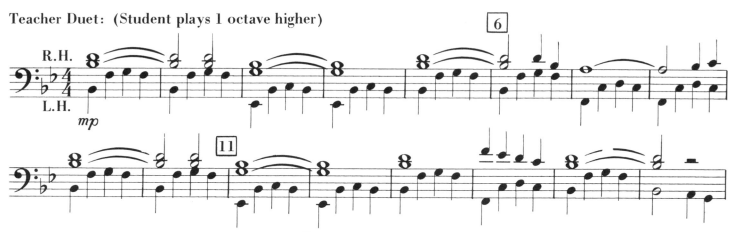

R.H.

L.H.

Come Thou Almighty King

Text — Anonymous
Tune — Felice de Giardini

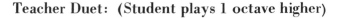

Teacher Duet: (Student plays 1 octave higher)

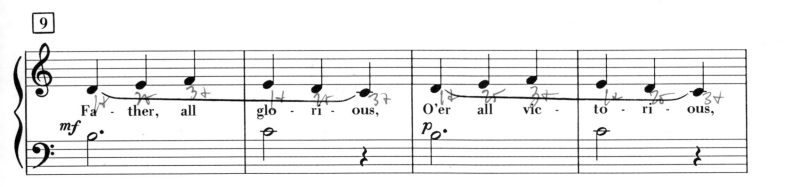

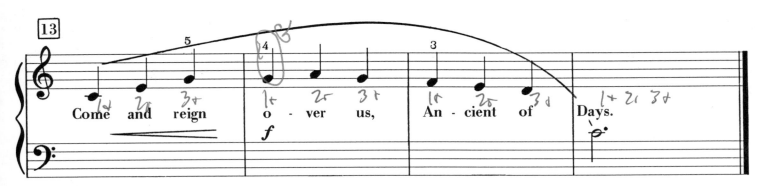

OVER →

Middle C Position

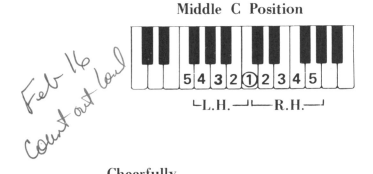

Feb 16
Count out loud

Great!

For the Beauty of the Earth

Text — F. Pierpoint
Tune — Conrad Kocher

Cheerfully

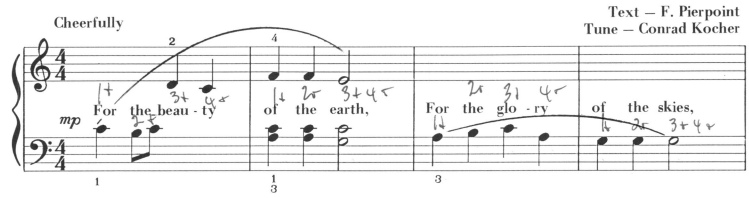

For the beau-ty of the earth, For the glo-ry of the skies,

For the love which from our birth O-ver and a-round us lies,

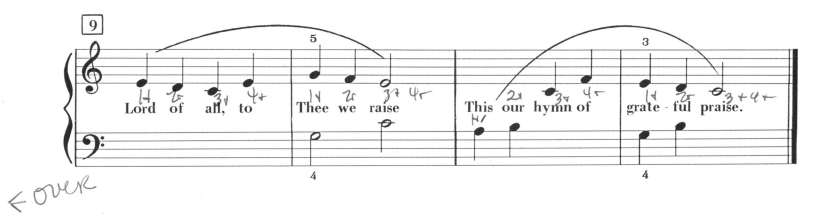

Lord of all, to Thee we raise This our hymn of grate-ful praise.

← OVER

Teacher Duet: (Student plays 1 octave higher)